DATE DUE

OCT 6 '78		
NOV 20 '79		
MAR 3 '80		
FEB 2 3 1993		
DEC 2 1 1995		
JAN 5 1996		

Compliments of:
PERMA-BOUND
HERTZBERG NEW METHOD, INC.
CHRYS MICKEL, REP.
1012 Arcturus (303) 475-0819
Colorado Springs, Colo. 80906

gordon parks

By MIDGE TURK   Illustrated by Herbert Danska

Today Gordon Parks is famous throughout the world as an outstanding photographer, but he began his life as the fifteenth son of a very poor black farmer in Kansas.

The family had barely enough money for food and clothes, and Gordon and his brothers fished in the river and trapped rabbits for dinner.

His mother felt that Gordon was special. She died when he was sixteen years old, but she left him with a valuable message: ". . . if a white boy can do something, so can you. Never give up trying to do your best."

Although he had to drop out of school to help support his brothers and sisters, and although at first had only a second-hand camera from a pawnshop, Gordon Parks never forgot his mother's words. The photographs he took were good.

Now he has produced his own successful full length movie. He has written several books. He was a staff photographer for *Life* magazine. But Gordon Parks will be best remembered for the beautiful, truthful photographs he has taken of black people in America.

Thomas Y. Crowell Company,
New York

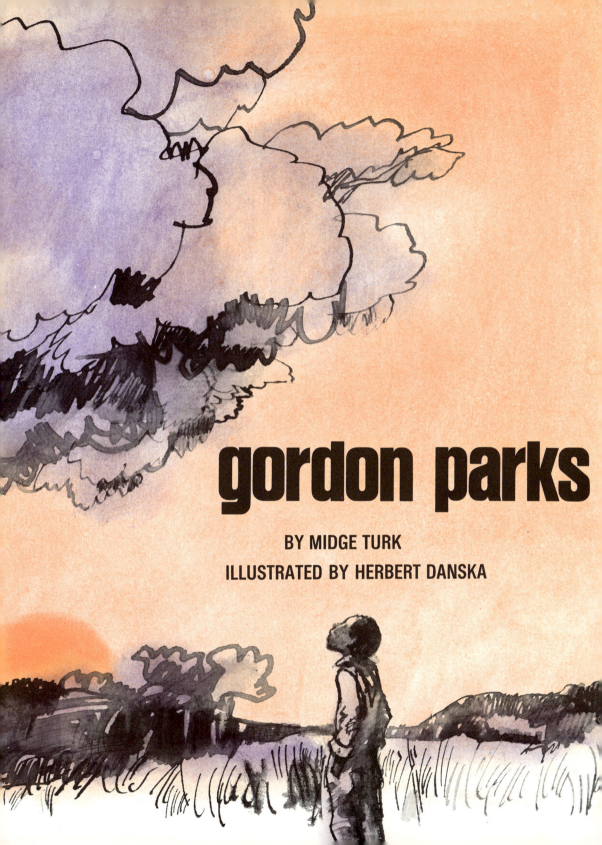

gordon parks

BY MIDGE TURK

ILLUSTRATED BY HERBERT DANSKA

Crowell Crocodiles are paperbacks selected from the highly recommended:

--- LET'S-READ-AND-FIND-OUT SCIENCE BOOKS ---

Editors:
Dr. Roma Gans, Professor Emeritus of Childhood Education, Teachers College, Columbia University
Dr. Franklyn M. Branley, Chairman and Astronomer of the American Museum—Hayden Planetarium

A Baby Starts to Grow   *My Visit to the Dinosaurs*
Bees and Beelines   *Oxygen Keeps You Alive*
A Drop of Blood   *Straight Hair, Curly Hair*
How a Seed Grows   *The Sunlit Sea*
It's Nesting Time   *What I Like About Toads*
My Five Senses   *What Makes Day and Night*

◀ YOUNG MATH BOOKS ▶

Editor: Dr. Max Beberman, Director of the Committee on School Mathematics Projects, University of Illinois

Bigger and Smaller   *Straight Lines, Parallel Lines,*
Estimation   *Perpendicular Lines*
Fractions Are Parts   *Weighing and Balancing*
*   of Things*   *What Is Symmetry?*

⤝ CROWELL BIOGRAPHIES ⤞

Editor: Susan Bartlett Weber

Cesar Chavez   *Malcolm X*
Eleanor Roosevelt   *Maria Tallchief*
Gordon Parks   *The Ringling Brothers*
Jim Thorpe   *Wilt Chamberlain*

1   2   3   4   5   6   7   8   9   10

CROWELL CROCODILE EDITION, 1973

gordon parks

CB A CROWELL BIOGRAPHY

On a small plot of brown earth near the center
of our country stands a little wooden house. In
this house, in Fort Scott, Kansas, Gordon Parks
was born. His Poppa was a strong man. He
planted potatoes, carrots, and beans on the land
behind his home. When the vegetables were ripe,
he picked them and sold them to his neighbors.

1

At other times he worked for a farmer who had a large farm. On his horse, Ribbon, Mr. Parks rounded up the farmer's cows and brought them to the barn each night.

Gordon's Momma was small but she worked hard. She asked for two things from her family. First, she wanted them to go to church with her on Sundays. Second, she asked them to tell her the truth at all times. She kept her house clean, cooked delicious meals, and cared for her children. There were seven boys and eight girls. Gordon was the youngest of all.

The Parks family was very poor. They had just enough money to buy food and some clothes. They gathered wood in the forest to keep their house warm in the cold winter. Gordon slept with four of his brothers in a tiny room.

Gordon's brothers taught him how to ride Ribbon. They also taught him to hunt and shoot possum in the woods near their home.

Sometimes they trapped for food, using a wooden box propped up at one end with a forked stick. They put a carrot under the box and tied a string to the stick. Then they hid in the bushes. When a rabbit nibbled the carrot, they jerked the string and the box fell, trapping the rabbit inside.

Gordon and his friends raided apple and peach orchards when the fruit was ready to eat. They

fished for perch in the river. On hot, sticky summer days they splashed in the cool water of the swimming hole.

At times Gordon saddled Ribbon and rode alone in the fields looking, listening, and dreaming. He imagined he was a cowboy being chased by Indians or a sheriff riding after outlaws.

Sometimes he got off his horse

and picked sweet, black mulberries to eat. Or he lay on the ground and watched June bugs crawl up blades of grass.

In Fort Scott, Gordon went to a school for black children. He learned to read and to work math problems. He listened to the stories his teacher told. Because he wanted to learn all he could, he did his work carefully.

The black people had their own church and they liked to sing their prayers. Gordon loved music. When he heard the organ music in the church, his toes danced inside his shoes.

One day when Gordon was seven years old, he heard a song in his head. It was like magic. Run-

ning to the tall piano in his house, he started to play the song. He was able to make it sound like the one in his head. After that, he often sat at the piano and played his own music or wrote songs in his notebook. In junior high school he joined the school band and learned to play the trombone. His parents were proud when Gordon played the solo at his graduation.

Sports were also a part of Gordon's life. His basketball team won most of its games. The boys wanted very much to play the white boys' team, but the white people in the town would not let them. Gordon began to understand that being black made a difference.

After the games the boys liked to drink sodas. One day Gordon and some of his teammates went into the white man's drugstore and sat at the counter. The white people glared at them. Minutes passed and no one waited on them. Finally, the man in charge asked the boys to leave. They wanted to fight back, but they were outnumbered. Gordon ran home with hot, angry tears streaming down his face.

"Gordon," his Momma said, "don't use your fists to fight the white man. You'll get hurt and into trouble. Fight with your brain. It's got a lot more power."

Gordon's mother knew that her youngest child was special. She felt that he would be a great man someday. She did not want Gordon to be discouraged because he was not white.

One afternoon Gordon came home from school to find his Momma in bed. The doctor was there. Gordon sat on the front steps with a sick feeling

in his stomach. "Your mother wants to see you,"
Mr. Parks softly called to his son. Gordon ran to
his Momma's bed and stood near her, holding
her hand. "Gordon," she said, "if a white boy
can do something, so can you. Never give up
trying to do your best."

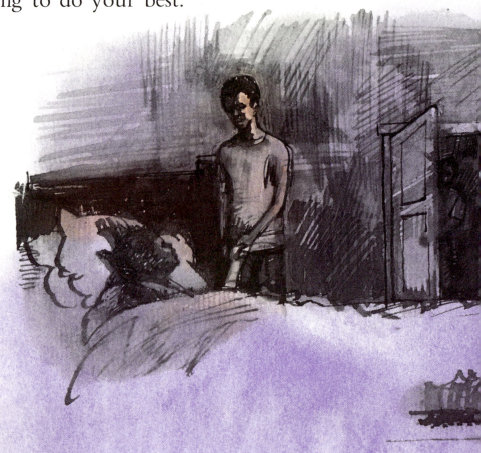

She died that night. Gordon was sixteen. He promised never to forget her dreams for him.

All his life Gordon had lived in Kansas with his family. That summer his father sent him many miles on a train to live with his married sister, Maggie Lee, in St. Paul, Minnesota. But her husband did not like having Gordon in the house. He was a man who did not like children and had none of his own. Gordon felt uneasy living there.

Gordon enrolled in high school. He played basketball and joined a boys' club. He was on his way to a meeting one evening when his brother-in-law stopped him. "Where're you going?" he asked angrily.

"To a club meeting," Gordon answered.

"No, you're not! You're staying home!"

Gordon wanted to go. His sister pleaded for him, but her husband shoved her aside and began to beat Gordon, pounding his head against the floor. He flung Gordon out of the house and threw his clothes and books out of the window into the snow. "Don't ever come back!" he shouted.

Gordon gathered his few belongings and trudged down the street. He was alone in the city without a place to eat and sleep, too ashamed to go to his friends for help.

For several months Gordon lived in a trolley car. Every evening he rode the trolley car between St. Paul and Minneapolis. He did his homework, and when he got sleepy, he curled up on the wooden seat. After school he worked in a diner and made enough money to pay the trolley fare and sometimes buy a meal of hot dogs and milk. Once in a while he slept with friends, and their mothers fed him. Some evenings Maggie Lee left him food in the milk box outside the back door. Yet Gordon grew thin. He was lonely and longed for his family, but he did not feel sorry for himself.

In summer Gordon's Poppa and some of his sisters and brothers moved to St. Paul. Maggie Lee helped them find Gordon. He was overjoyed to be with them again. But the Parks family was still poor, and Gordon had to stop school and work. Whenever he could find time, he read books from the public library and wrote songs in his notebook. He never got a chance to go back to school again.

When he was twenty-one, Gordon married his high school sweetheart, Sally. To earn money he got a job as a porter on a train. The train took him to many big cities. When he was in Chicago, something important happened. He went to a motion picture theater and heard a famous photographer, Norman Alley, speak. Mr. Alley showed some of the exciting movies he had made.

Suddenly Gordon became aware of all the things that pictures can say. He sat through another show, and before he left the theater, he had made up his mind to become a photographer.

Gordon bought his first camera in a pawnshop in Seattle. Eagerly, he hurried to the harbor and

walked out on a pier. While taking pictures of
sea gulls floating high in the air, he slipped and
fell into the water. Firemen in a nearby station
heard his yells and pulled him out. To Gordon's
surprise the pictures he took were good.

Gordon studied the photographs in magazines.
He read books that explained how to take good
pictures. And he took picture after picture. He
found that he liked to photograph old people,
close-ups of their heads and hands. He photographed pretty girls who wanted to be models.
He photographed farm lands, lakes, boats, flowers,
trees. People began to notice his work. He was
able to sell some of his pictures.

By now Gordon and his wife had two children, Gordon and Toni. He left his train job and
moved his family to Chicago. There he earned
money photographing rich society women. But
he spent his free time taking pictures on Chicago's South Side where the black people live.
Gordon's pictures showed how poor the black

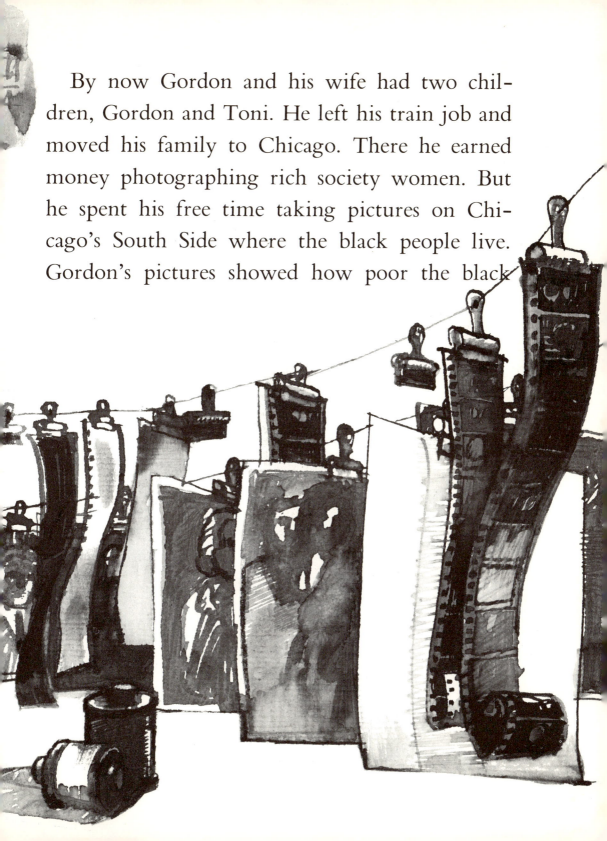

people are. He wanted everyone to see the way the black man has to live.

At the end of that year Gordon's photographs were shown at the South Side Community Art Center. The exhibit won an award. With the money he decided to learn more about photography.

He took his family and went to Washington, D.C., to study with a famous teacher. His name was Roy Stryker. The first day he told Gordon to walk around the city and see how a Negro is treated. Gordon was surprised, but he left the office and started down the street.

Soon he felt hungry and went into a cafeteria to eat lunch. "Colored people are not served here," the manager told him.

Next he walked into a large clothing store. "I want to buy an overcoat," he said politely. The salesman asked him to wait. For a half hour Gordon watched the salesman help white customers.

Then he spoke to the salesman again. He was refused help.

Later he tried to buy a ticket to the movies. The girl at the ticket window shook her head. "Colored people are not permitted inside," she said.

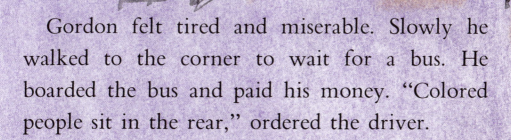

Gordon felt tired and miserable. Slowly he walked to the corner to wait for a bus. He boarded the bus and paid his money. "Colored people sit in the rear," ordered the driver.

The next day Roy Stryker asked, "What did you learn?" Gordon told him. Then Mr. Stryker asked, "Can you tell it without words?" Gordon spent the next year taking pictures that told what the black man suffers.

Gordon tried to keep from hating the white people who disliked Negroes. He knew that he must fight for himself and every black man in the way he knew best. Through his pictures he would tell the world about the black man.

When Gordon's year of study was over, he moved his family again. This time they went to New York City. Gordon and his wife now had a third child, a baby boy, David. Their new home was a few crowded rooms in Harlem, a section of

the city where black people live. The two older children, Gordon and Toni, played among the garbage cans in the dirty streets in front of their tenement. Gordon did not like it, but there was no other place Negroes could rent rooms.

Finally Gordon sold some of his pictures to *Life* Magazine. He was well paid for his work. Soon after that the magazine hired Gordon to take all kinds of pictures. At last Gordon had the kind of job he wanted. For the next twenty years, he traveled all over the United States. He also went to South America, to Europe, and to Japan. He took pictures of important black people, of children from many countries, and of kings and queens. He also took pictures of fashion models

wearing beautiful new clothes. But the most important pictures he made were of a family in
Harlem.

In this family were eight children. They lived
with their mother and father in three tiny rooms.

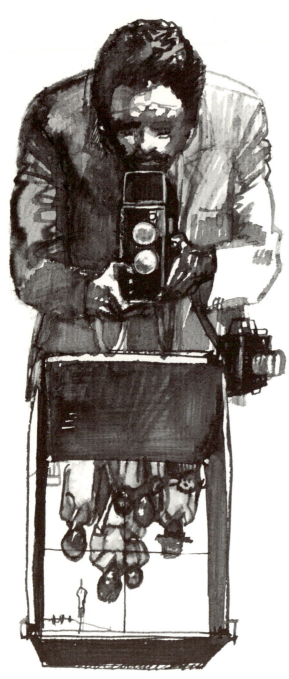

To keep warm on cold winter nights, they dragged mattresses into the kitchen and slept together on the floor near the stove. The windows were broken, and rats crawled in and out of the holes in the walls. The children kept their clothes in cardboard cartons because there were no closets. Usually the family shared a small piece of stale fish for dinner because it was all they had.

Gordon spent many days and nights with the family taking pictures. His pictures showed tears in the father's eyes and sadness in the mother's face. They showed the thin, hungry children.

Gordon wrote a story to go with the pictures. White people, he wrote, have kept black people poor. Gordon told why the father was not working. He had been fired so that a white man could have his job. Gordon asked the white people to find work for this man and other black men. He asked for better houses for black families to live in. He asked white people to care about black people.

Millions of people read the story and saw Gordon's pictures. Many white people wrote to tell Gordon they were going to help the Negroes who lived in their cities. They said they understood black people better now.

Gordon Parks was not satisfied just taking photographs and writing about them. He wrote music as well. He loved music and listened to records while he wrote his stories. When he finished writing, he often sat at his piano and composed. Over the years his music was played by orchestras in the United States, Italy, and Germany.

Gordon also wrote books. His first book was called *The Learning Tree*. It told how a young black boy felt while growing up among white people who were unkind to him.

Three years later he wrote another book, *A Choice of Weapons*. It was also about his own life. It told how Gordon chose to fight the white man's prejudice with love and hard work rather than his fists.

"My work gets the bitterness out of me," Gordon said. "I say what I can in photography. When that's not enough, I turn to writing music, poetry or novels." Some of Gordon's poems and photographs were put together in a beautiful book called *A Poet and His Camera*. His books have been read by many people in this country. They have also been translated into other languages and read by people all over the world.

By now Gordon Parks was a famous man. Yet he had another dream. Ever since he had written *The Learning Tree,* he wanted to make it into a film. Finally a Hollywood motion picture studio let him. He wrote the music as well. He was the first Negro to produce and direct a movie for a

big company. Now he hopes other black men
will be able to do the same thing.

Gordon Parks is a gentle, quiet man who speaks

softly. He has a friendly face with brown eyes, a large gray mustache, and gray-black hair. Often he is so busy that he forgets what time it is. Then his family and friends see very little of him. Other times, he spends weekends playing tennis or riding Champ, a sleek brown horse his family gave him for Christmas. His two sons, Gordon and David, have grown up to be photographers. Toni, like her father, is interested in music.

Gordon has made many friends through his work. When he walks down the street in New York, people recognize him and smile. They recognize him in Hollywood, too, and Paris, and other places where he has been with his camera.

He has received awards for his pictures from the Philadelphia Museum of Art and from the Photographic Society of America. Other groups have honored him for helping black and white people understand each other better. Harvard University and Boston University have given

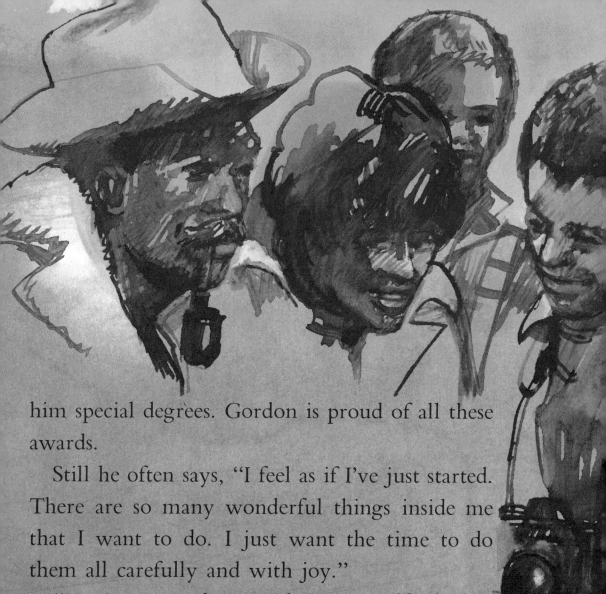

him special degrees. Gordon is proud of all these awards.

Still he often says, "I feel as if I've just started. There are so many wonderful things inside me that I want to do. I just want the time to do them all carefully and with joy."

"You've got to have pride in yourself," he believes. "You have to keep searching to find a way to win at life." Gordon is a happy man because he found the way.

33

ABOUT THE AUTHOR

Midge Turk has been an elementary school teacher, a high school teacher, a high school principal, and Dean's Assistant at New York University. She is presently College Editor at *Glamour* Magazine. Born in Los Angeles, California, she now makes her home in New York City.

Miss Turk met Gordon Parks during her first year at *Glamour,* when she was assigned to work with him on a story for which he took the photographs. They have been good friends ever since then.

ABOUT THE ILLUSTRATOR

As a writer-director of motion pictures, graphic artist and author Herbert Danska naturally feels "an affinity to the range of Gordon Parks' creative activities."

Mr. Danska has illustrated some eighteen books, including one that he also wrote, *The Street Kids,* a novel for young readers. His documentary and dramatic films have received two Golden Eagles from *Cine,* and awards at many world film festivals. *Right On!,* his latest feature, won the International Film Critics Prize, 1970.

While working in a number of places abroad, Mr. Danska makes his home with his wife and two children in New York.